Voice of the Feminine I Am

Innocent to Enlightened
A collection of original illustrated poetry

CHARLOTTA ORNELAS

BALBOA.PRESS
A DIVISION OF HAY HOUSE

Balboa Press books may be ordered through booksellers or by contacting:

Balboa Press
A Division of Hay House
1663 Liberty Drive
Bloomington, IN 47403
www.balboapress.com
1 (877) 407-4847

Interior Image Credit: Charlotta Ornelas

Print information available on the last page.

ISBN: 978-1-9822-4676-1 (sc)
ISBN: 978-1-9822-4675-4 (hc)
ISBN: 978-1-9822-4674-7 (e)

Library of Congress Control Number: 2020907072

Balboa Press rev. date: 04/29/2020

Voice of the Feminine I Am

Innocent to Enlightened

A Collection of Original Illustrated Poems

Dedication

This book is dedicated to my family

whom inspired me to all my art.

Jose my husband "Big Love"

Camilla and Josefine my daughters

"Mothers Words"

Britt-Marie my mother "Atelje Rose"

Bo my maternal grandpa "Soft Whisper"

Anna-Stina my maternal

grandma "Fragile Bones"

Note to the Reader

I wrote and made my illustrations for this book with thought of being a cat with 9 lives. As a woman we go through life in stages where we grow through trials and experiences. Each chapter of this book is laid out in 9 stages and I want the reader to reflect on the stage the poem is written in. My illustrations will further capture the intention and mood of the poetry. This book includes 5 chapters of poetry and each chapter has a theme running through it that reflects my experience with society and life in general.

LEDGER

Introduction to the Author

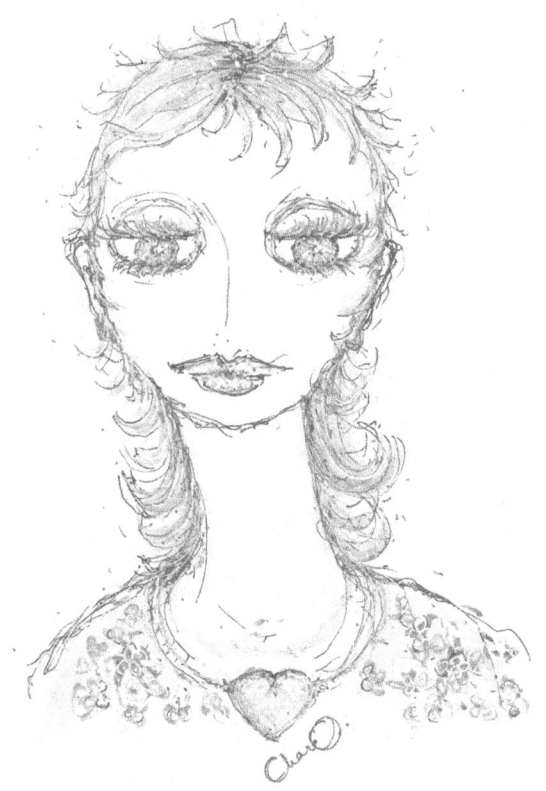

-*I Am*-

-I Am -

Innocent girl

A learning student

Teenage seduction

Exploring the world

Loving companion

A nurturing mother

Accepted journey

Woman transformation

Enlightened finally

Purpose of the Book

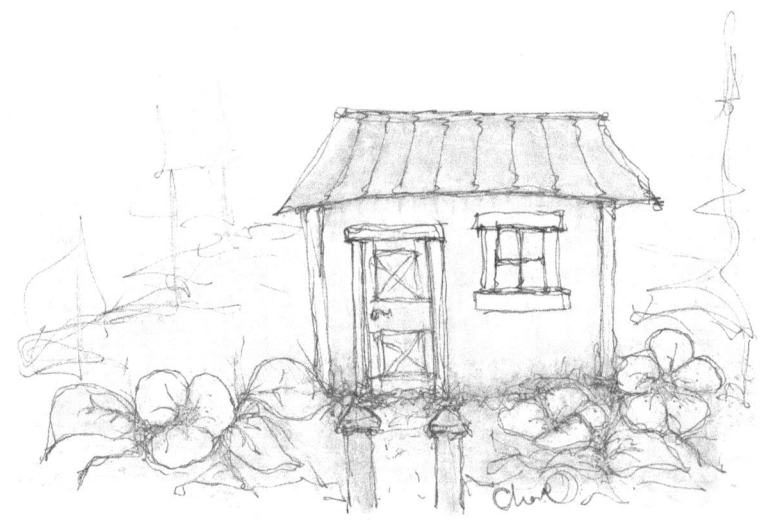

-Atelje Rose-

-Atelje Rose -

Blooms and petals shield

A dream comes true

Many years in waiting

For a healing touch

Now you have purpose

Holding treasures

Ready to be shared

Flowering at last

Inspirational Theme

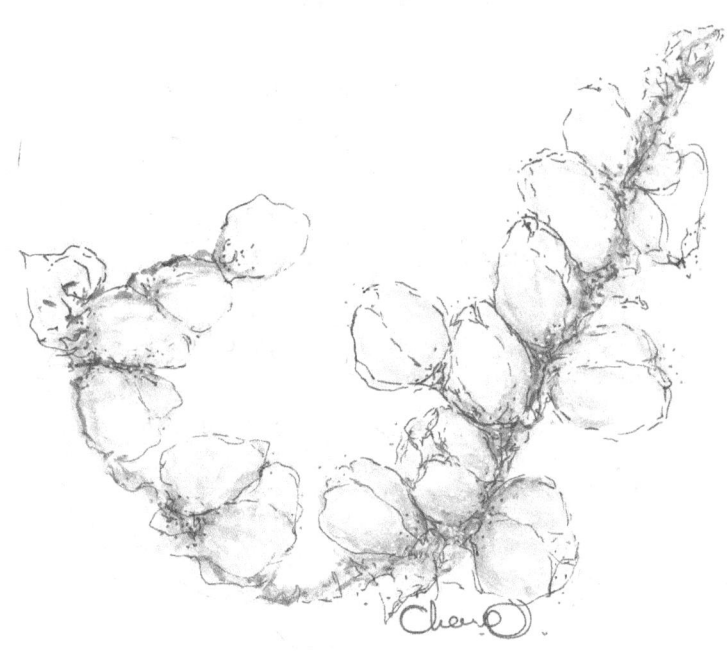

-Rose Torn -

-Rose Torn -

Soft and gentle

Looks deceiving

Underneath the sharp

Viciously penetrate

Caring to bleed

Heal your wound

Nurture your soul

To pain no other

Innocent Phase

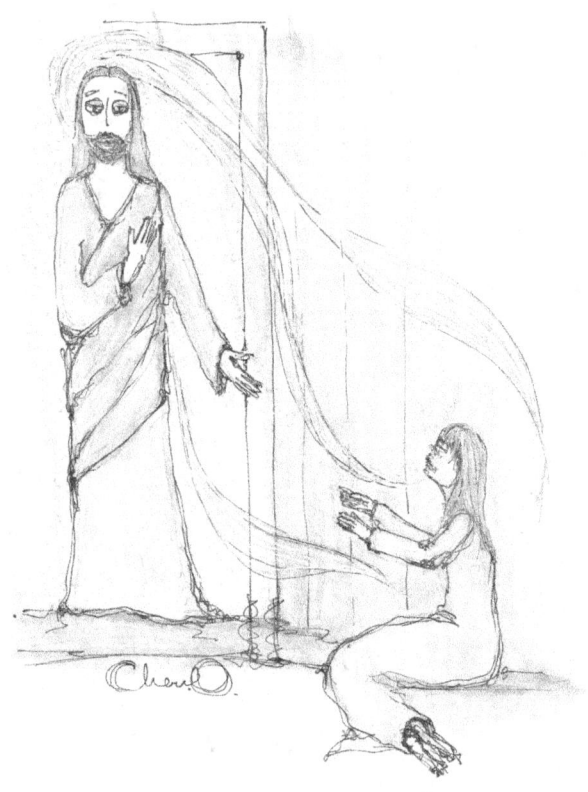

-Shattered Innocence-

-Shattered Innocence-

Mothers fury explode

Fathers silence accepting

Little girl confused thoughts

Future blurred

Robed presence approach softly

Comforting words

Do not worry

I will be with you always

Learner Phase

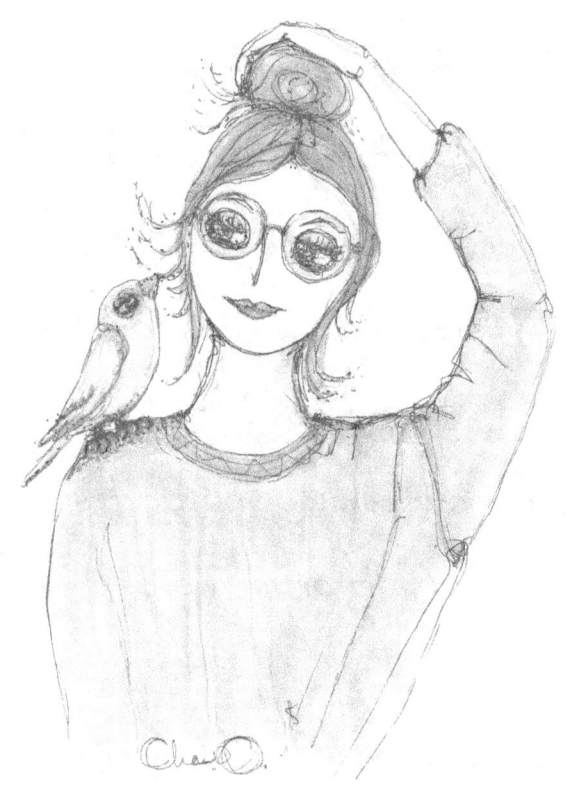

-Wisdom Whispers-

-Wisdom Whispers-

To too late

I wish I knew then

What I know now

You foolish youth

Many wasted years

This world is

Not for you

Seducer Phase

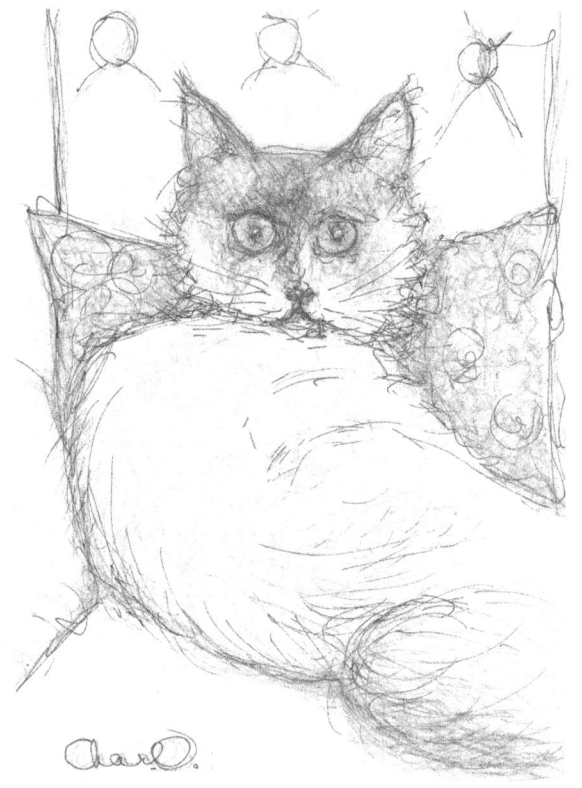

-Silky Lint-

-Silky Lint-

Fingertips caress

Piercing ice blue begging

Deep the little engine roars

Feline power

Swerves away

Longing

Explorer Phase

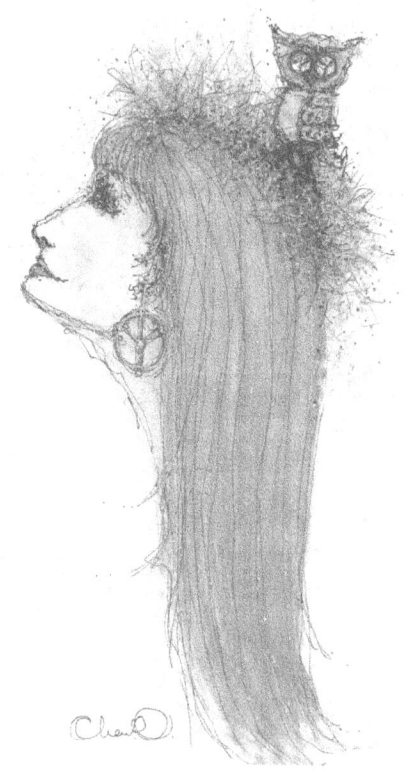

-World View-

-World View-

Peaceful interaction

Cultures carry wisdom

Native tongues

Understood in your gaze

Reach of your hand

Tone of your voice

Words mean nothing

I feel you

By touch

Lover Phase

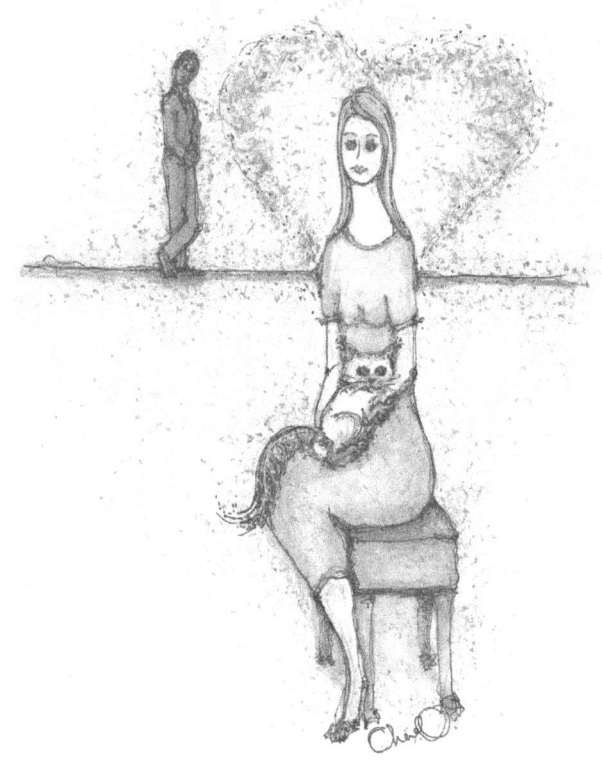

-Love Switch-

-Love Switch-

My soul nurtured

Soft pelt

Needy eyes

Who comes first

Prioritize

Back and forth

Switch love

Nurturer Phase

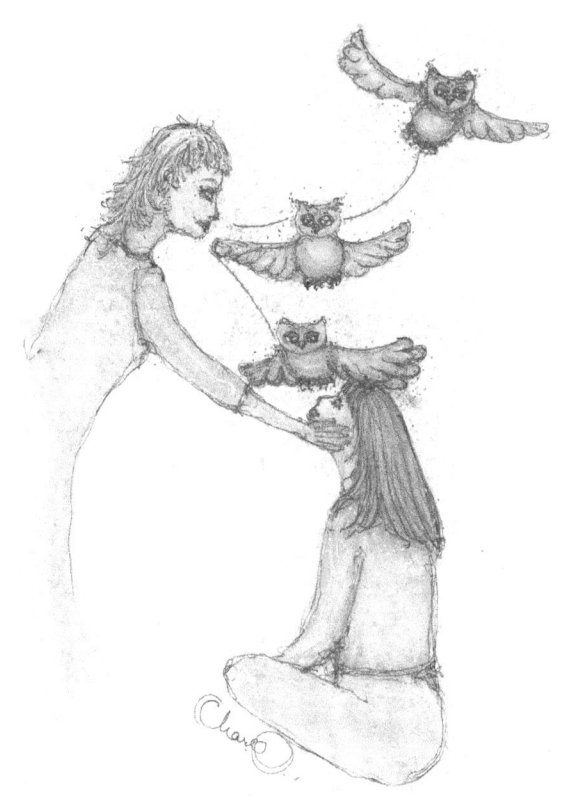

-Mothers Words-

-Mothers Words-

Child will you listen

I have been there

Trust in me

Your path I walked

Remember my words

When potholes appear

I know how

To keep clear

Acceptance Phase

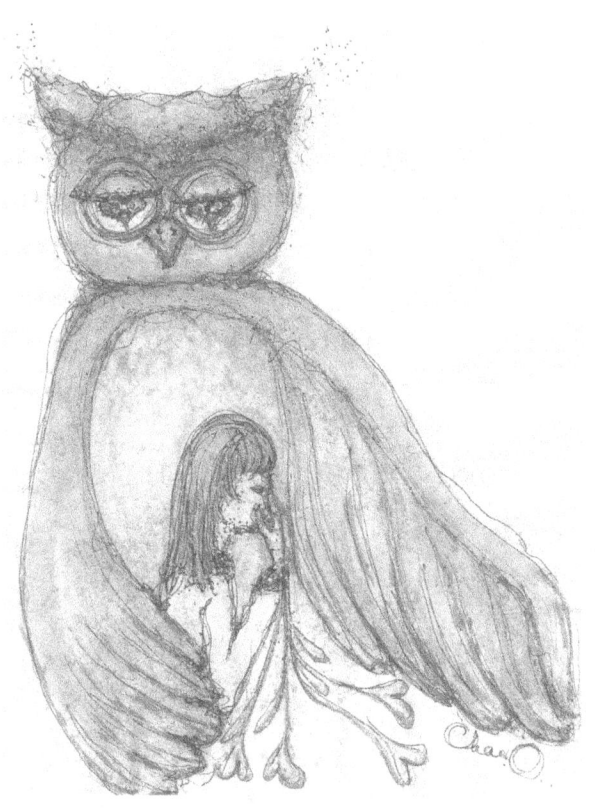

-Big Love-

-Big Love-

Make me weak

Embraces my whole being

I have to yield

Such scary surrender

Will I survive

Weeping tears of joy

It is worth

All the sorrow

That might follow

Transform Phase

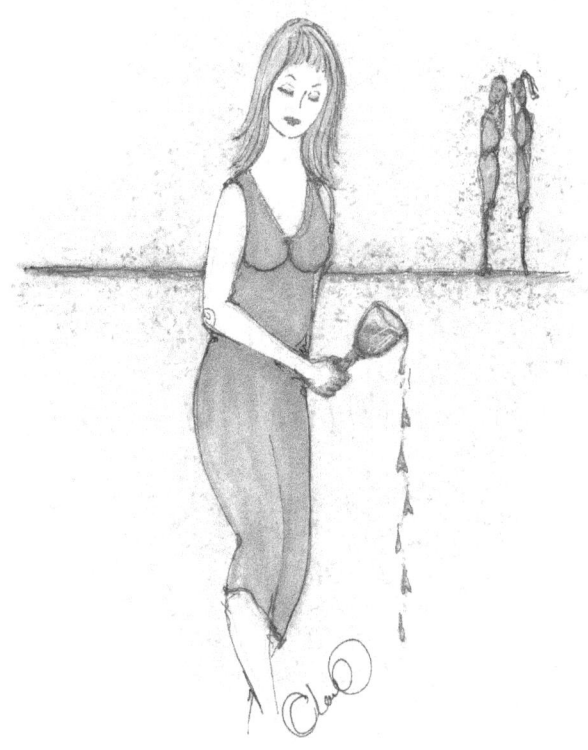

-Heavy Heart-

-Heavy Heart-

My dress too tight

Red velvet

Liquid gold

Cannot help me anymore

I feel heavy

Body and soul

Bring me back

To how I was before

Enlightenment Phase

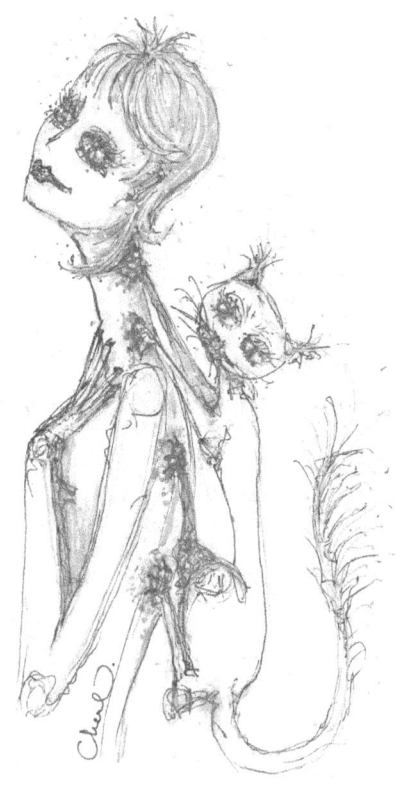

-Feline Now-

-Feline Now-

Became a part of me

Gratefully yours

Strength through trials

A woman vice

Too many paths taken

Many obligations

Claw your way out

Independence

Inspirational Theme

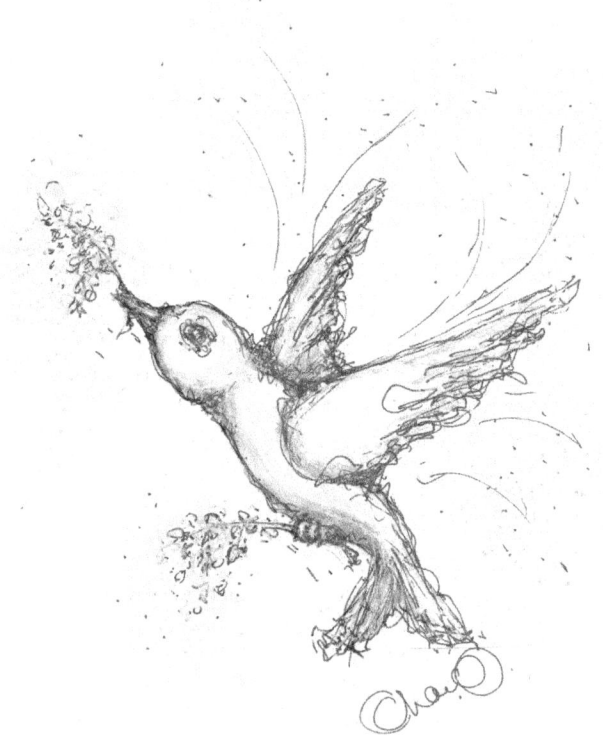

-Empath Winged-

-Empath Winged-

Blue feather light

Nothing but mist

Wings shimmer

Intentions fly

Breezes to eager ear

Listen to me

Secrets are told

Wasted

In the wind

Innocent Phase

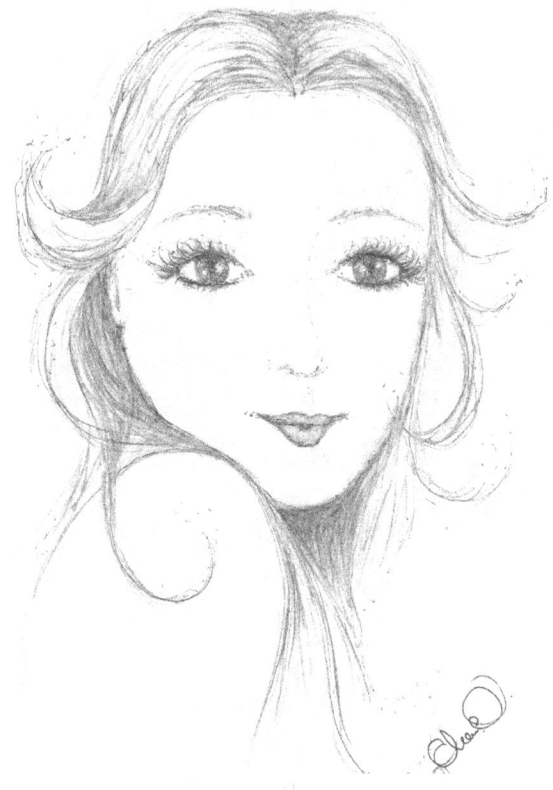

-Ocean Eyes-

-Ocean Eyes-

So vast and open

Horizon far away

Hopeful about life

No tears

Have fallen yet

Salt to earth

Skin without scars

No wounds have ben licked

Wish it could last

Innocence forever

Learner Phase

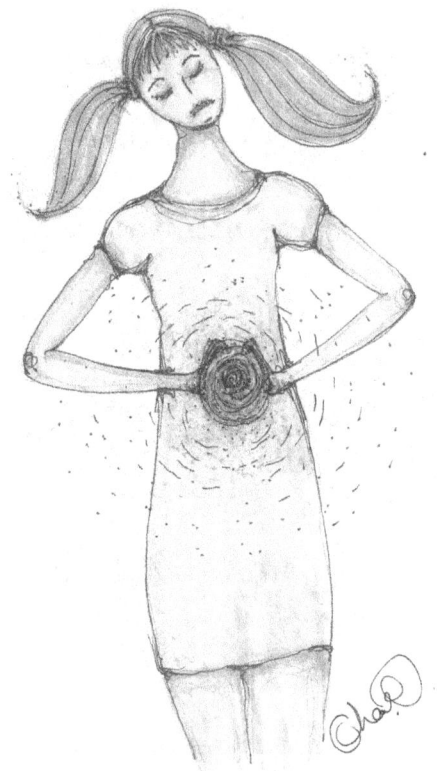

-Spirit Twist-

-Spirit Twist-

Early school daze

Hallway buzzles

Tall bodies

Bright light

Out of no where

Fist of exploding pain

Belly churns

For a little girl

No protection

Long suffering

Leaves a wound

Surgically removed

Later in life

Seducer Phase

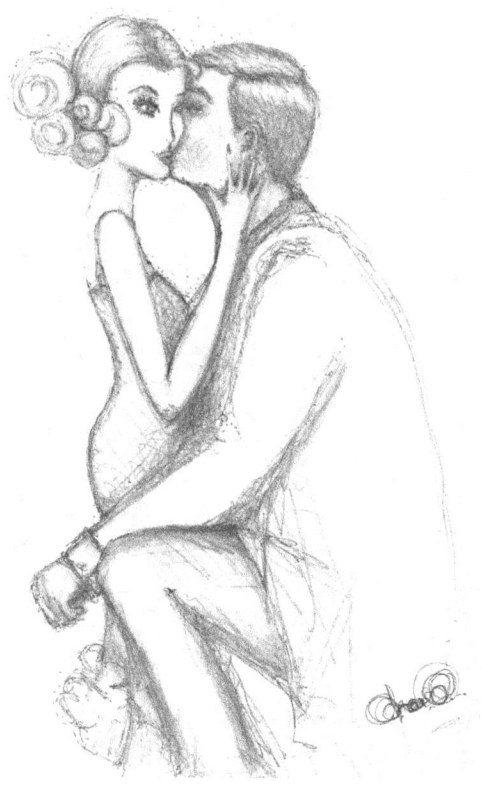

-Sweet Desire-

-Sweet Desire-

Rough skin

My curves are yielding

A chest so strong

Heart to heart

Fire is burning

Electric shock

When breaths exchange

Desired outcome

Explorer Phase

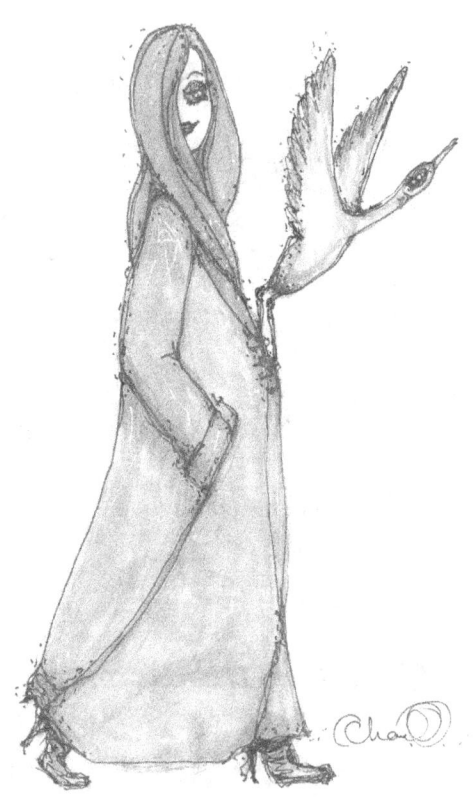

~Going Where~

-Going Where-

Lead me astray

Take me away

I am in need of

A tour guide

My feet are busy

Going no where

My destination

Are you out there

A life of travel

Will I ever arrive

Lover Phase

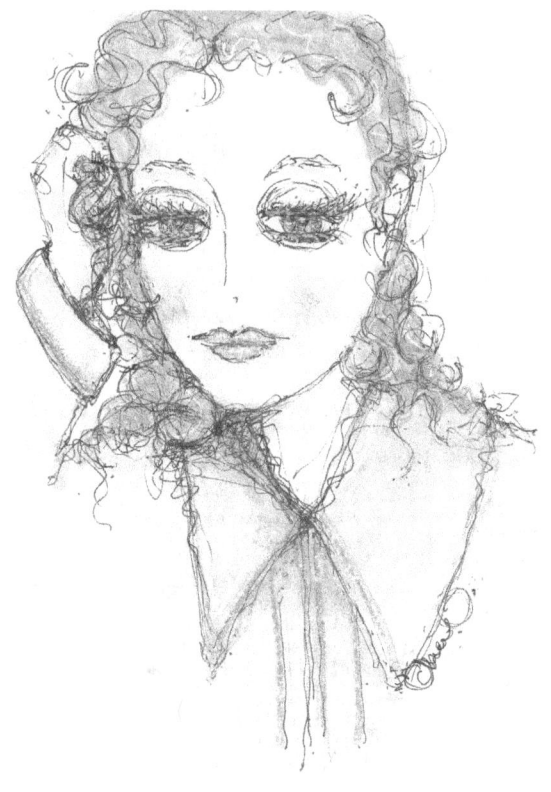

-Waiting For-

-Waiting For-

Why am I still

Here waiting

I am not willing

Waiting frustrated

Chest churns

Waiting

Red flash behind my eyes

Waiting NO more

Nurturer Phase

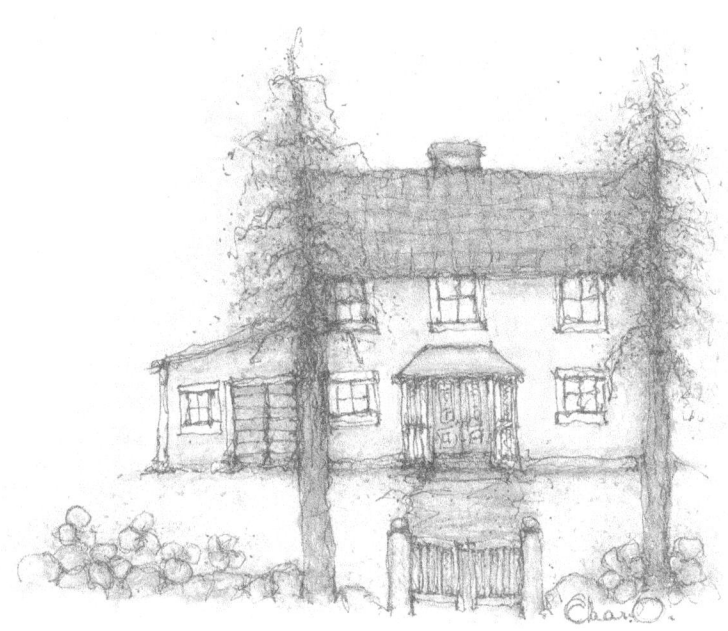

-Cottage Castle-

-Cottage Castle-

My little house

So worn

Safe in nature

Heavy trunks and stone

Green pastures embrace

Shabby old

Leaves crown your entrance

Antique

Leaning weary

Home is home

Acceptance Phase

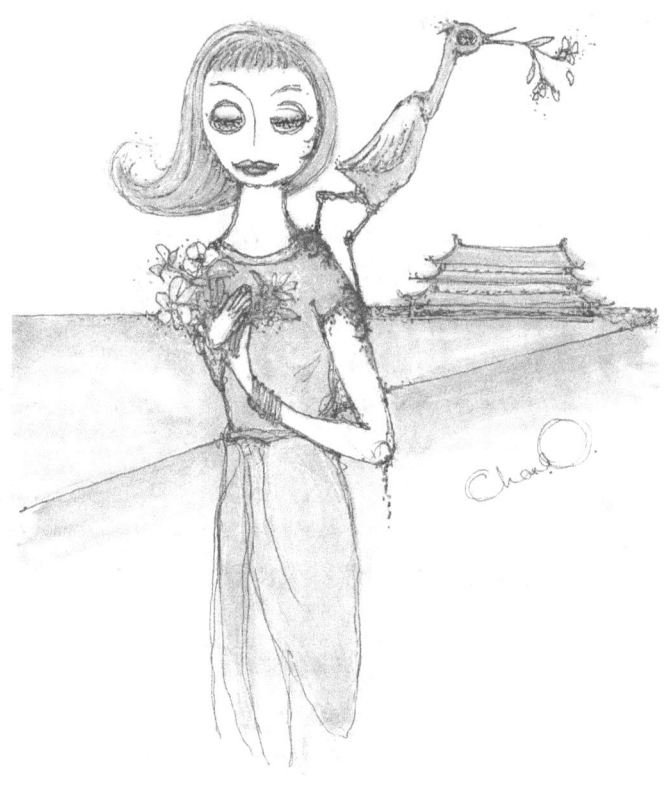

-Not celebrated-

-Not celebrated-

I worked so hard

Why does no one see

Take my trophies

It does not matter

Graduation

After graduation

No one came

Now it is over

I am retiring

Transform Phase

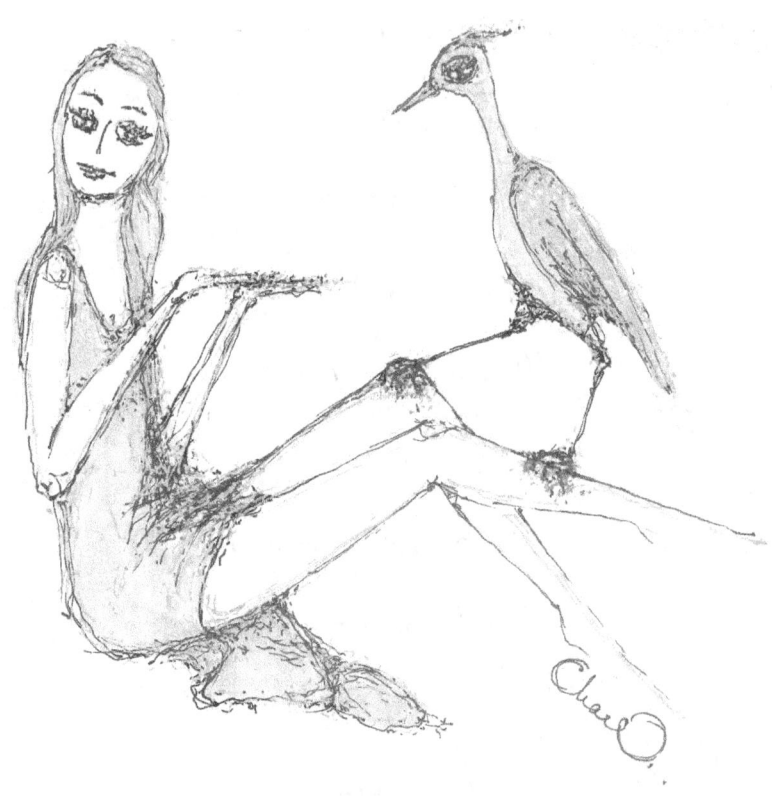

-Feminine Calling-

-Feminine Calling-

Dance in the wind

Sing chant call out

Swirl spin jump

Smooth curve

Long legs

Spirit trailing follow

Synchronized

Energy emerging

Fatal unity

Enlightenment Phase

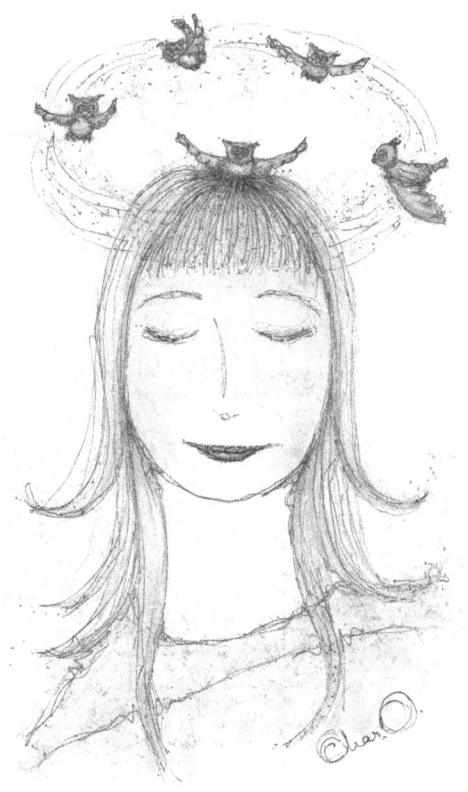

-Get Out-

-Get Out-

About my head

So grateful

This lightness inside

An electric source

Running up my spine

Exploding

Flowing around

Spinning my mind

Into the universe

Inspirational Theme

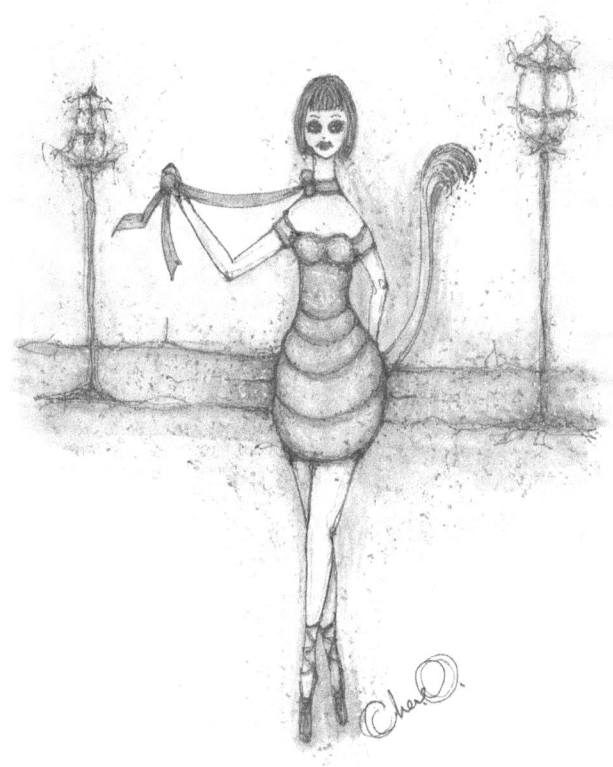

-Feline Phases-

-Feline Phases-

Nine lives to use

Pet on a string

Female petting zoo

Predators every where

Night life rules

Ladies

Learn the game

Achieve rank

Feminine carnage

Innocent Phase

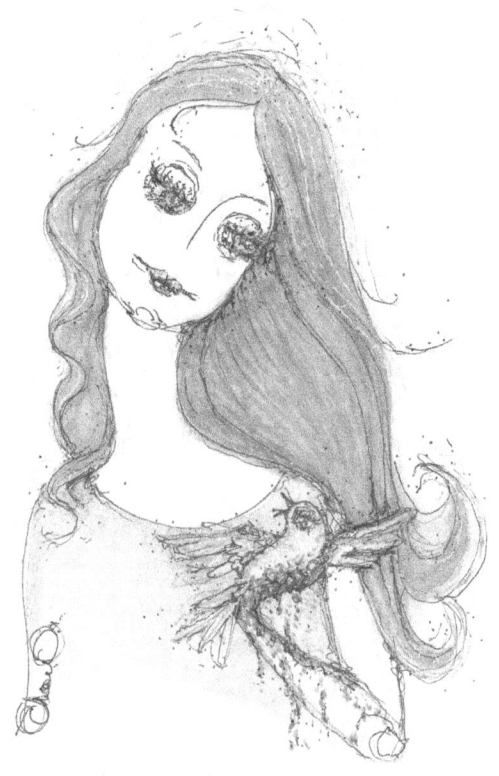

-Be Nice-

-Be Nice-

Little girl trusting

Always told

Respect elders

Slid away with a smile

Safe but furious

Feelings so raw

Where was my courage

Desired vindication

A woman lessons

Capable of confrontation

Maybe

In the future

Learner Phase

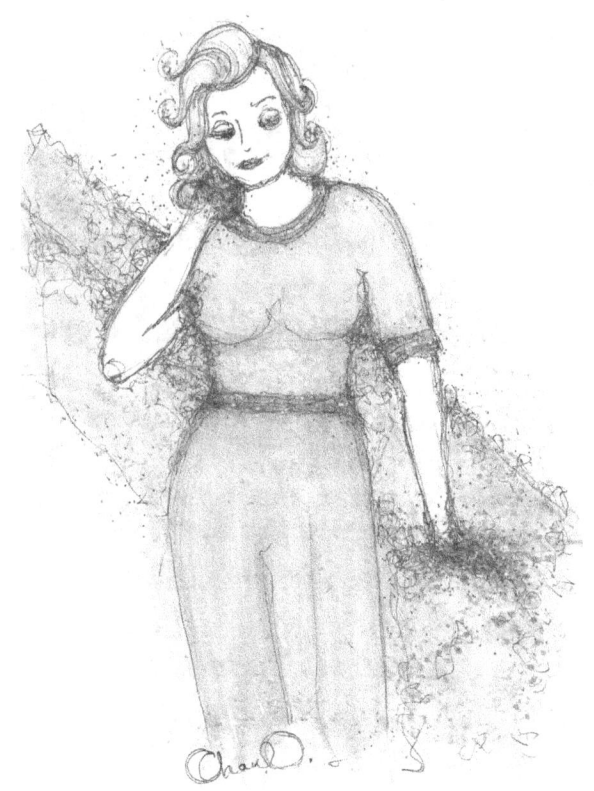

-Nature Calls-

-Nature Calls-

Springs cool breeze

Warm rays

Kiss my skin

Summertime lurking

Tugging at the days

Green blisters on all plants

Little explosions

Fragrance blossoms

Red all over

Seducer Phase

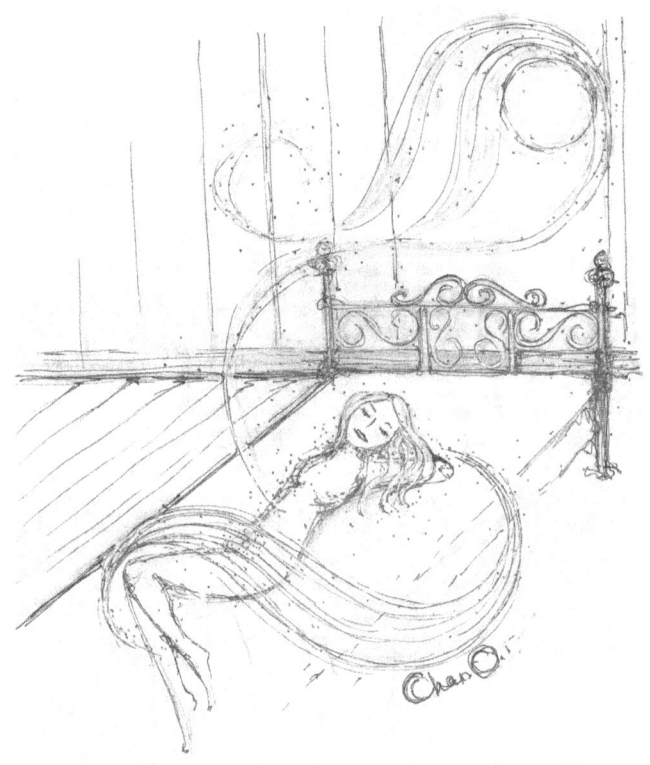

-Liquid Blue-

-Liquid Blue-

Darkness slivers

Silver beams through

Window curtains

Ticking faces

Curving numbers threesome

Eyes open wide

Mind swirling endless

Wishing for an audience

Only God

Is listening now

Explorer Phase

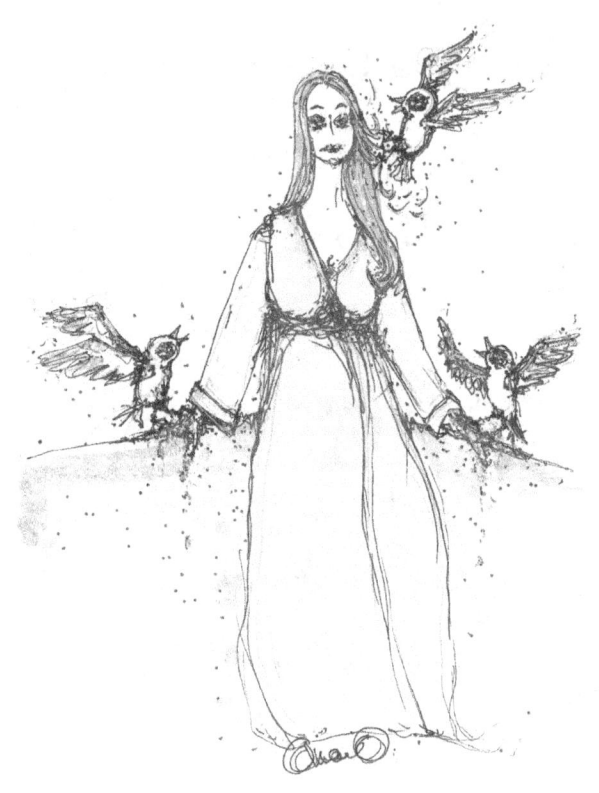

-Fuzzy Friends-

-Fuzzy Friends-

Pulled in all directions

Feelings of confusion

A price to pay

Customs so unexpected

Lost and found

New experiences

Builds confidence

Comes back home

Stronger than before

Lover Phase

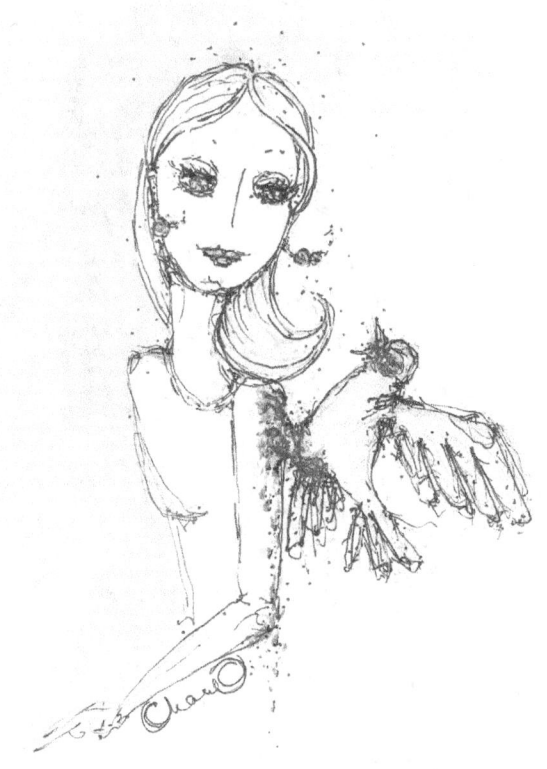

-Love Hurts-

-Love Hurts-

Digging

Into your skin

Always hoping

Beginning so lovely

Ugly shows her face

Chipping away

Connection is cut

Slowly the heart shrinks

Accepting what is

Nurturer Phase

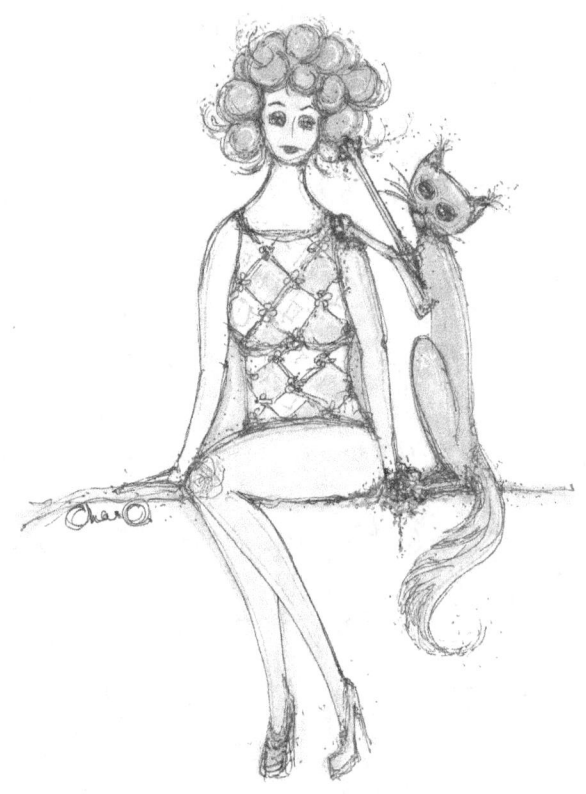

-Never Enough-

-Never Enough-

You always want more

Pulling my strings

Manipulation

Only nice

Until needs are met

What about me

My needs

You shy away

Again

Acceptance Phase

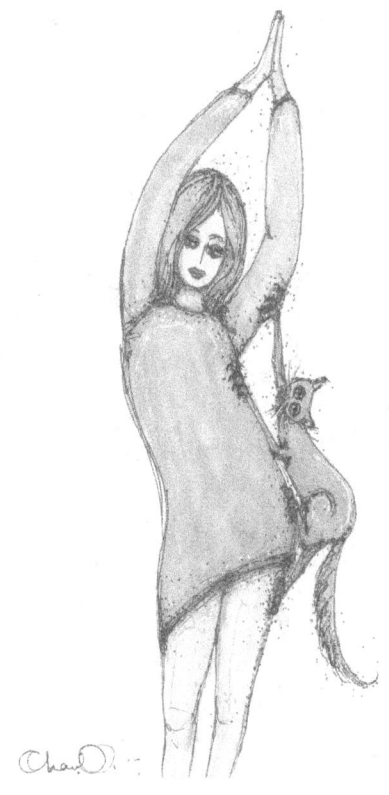

-Hidden Shadow-

-Hidden Shadow-

My alter self

Sub consciousness

Always

Pulling my insides

I know now

That you are

My only savior

It took a long time

Not to be afraid

Of the dark

Transform Phase

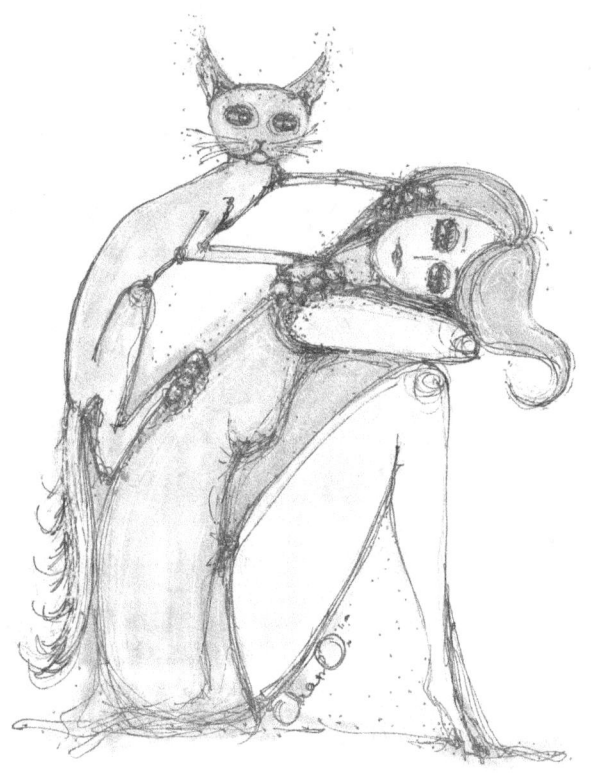

~Power Kills~

-Power Kills-

Feminine shows her claws

Demand attention

Do not step back

I fought so hard

For your strength

Red liquid sacrificed

Killing the bondage

Lessons of no use

Erasing the past

Enlightenment Phase

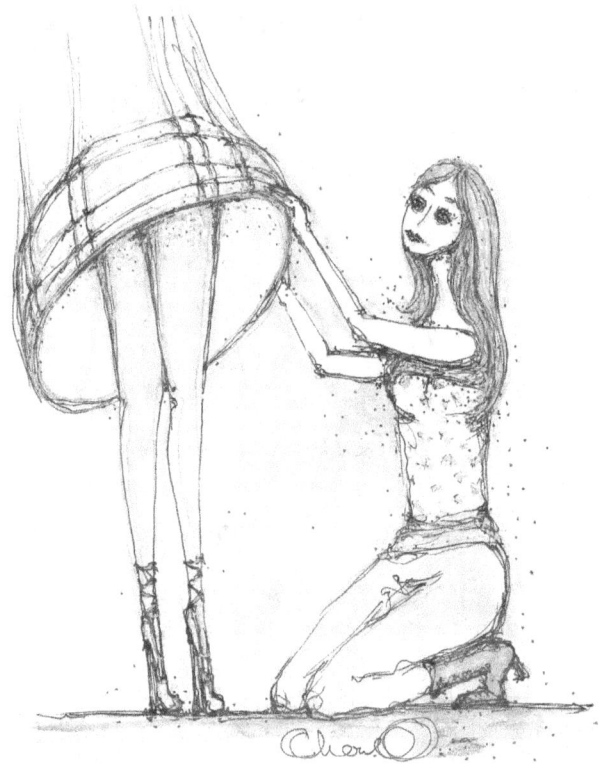

-Femme Fatale-

-Femme Fatale-

Kitty cat woman

Cannot tame my world

Do not alter

Mother nature

Alpha female

Eyeing her gene pool

A woman duty

To make sure

By serving

With no reward

The world turns

Inspirational Theme

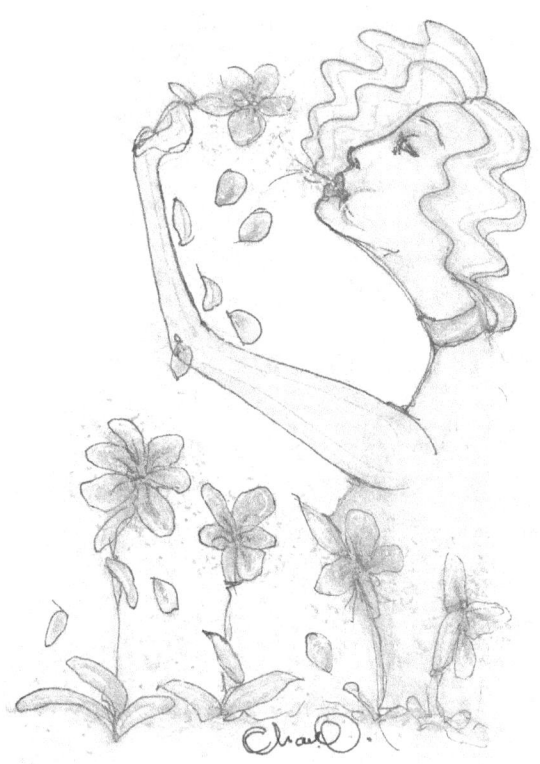

-Female Voice-

-Female Voice-

Breathing spirit

Heart chakra green

Mother earths full body

Naked and clean

To all a nurturer

Bosom so strong

Bountiful love

Never ending

Innocent Phase

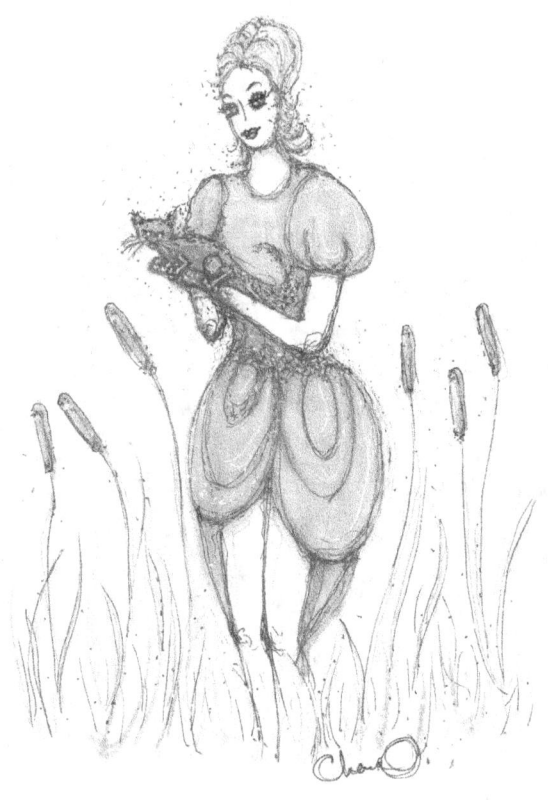

-Adorable Thing-

-Adorable Thing-

Silky and soft

Smooth curves

My little precious

So innocent

Only wants to caress

Take care of

Shield and protect

Will someone do the same

Care for you

Little princess

Learner Phase

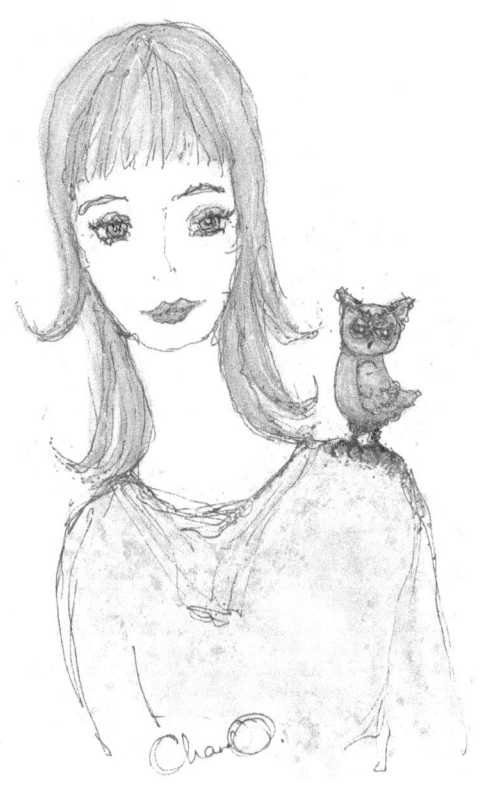

-Soft Whisper-

-Soft Whisper-

Wisdom words flow

Old knowledge

Share with me owl

Ancient tales told

Passed on from grands

To guide me

My favorite place

Their nest

Seducer Phase

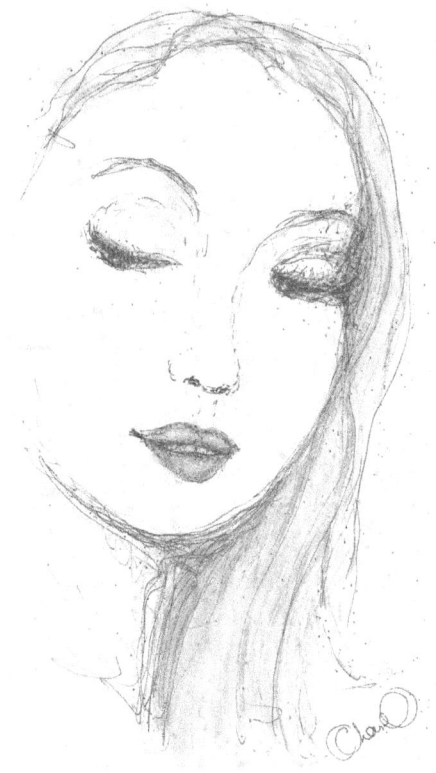

-Rosy Lips-

-Rosy Lips-

Red provokes

Passionate glossy

Alarming color

Enhances feminine power

A calling card

Attention to attractions

She has painted

Her intention

Explorer Phase

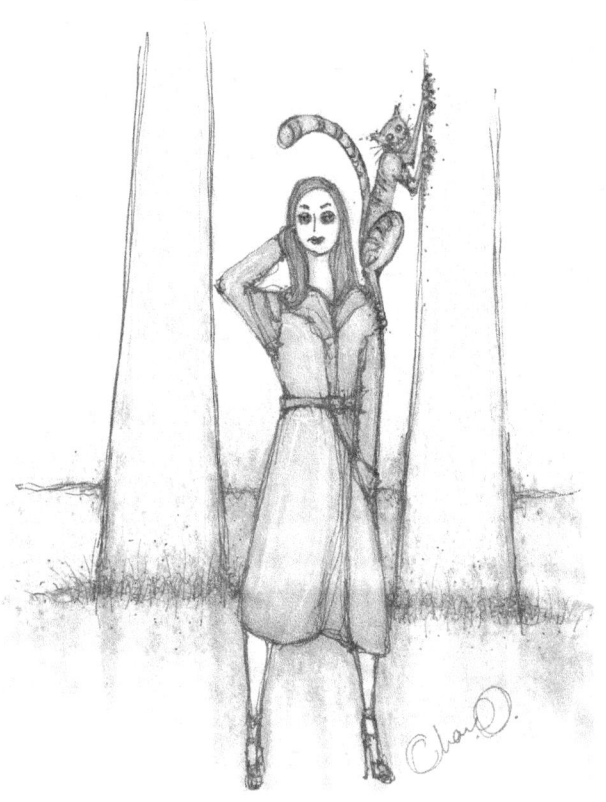

-You Know-

-You Know-

Where to go

With courage

All roads will lead

To your path

Do not get sidetracked

Avoid all traps

Follow your heart

To your destination

Lover Phase

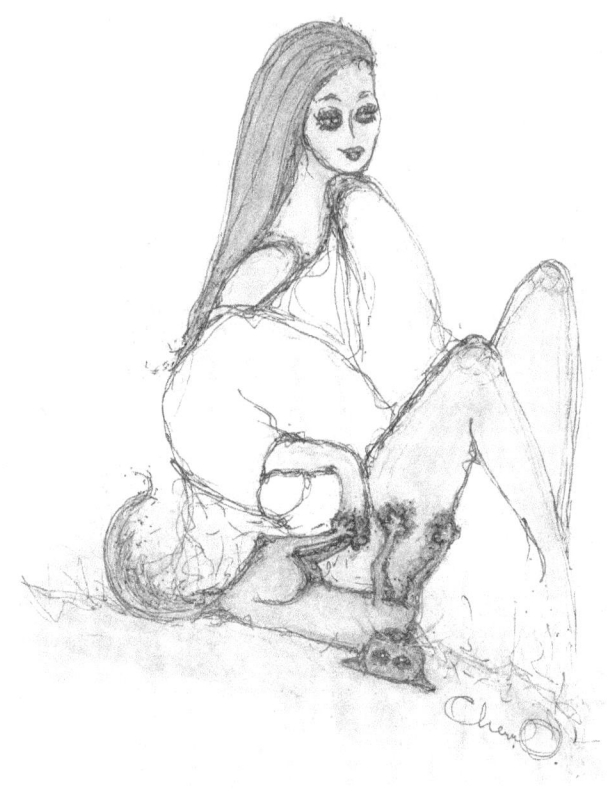

-Sitting Down-

-Sitting Down-

Letting you play

Here with me

Why so

This love is blind

Do you feel me

Not just my body

My needs

Do you see me

Not just my face

My soul

Nurturer Phase

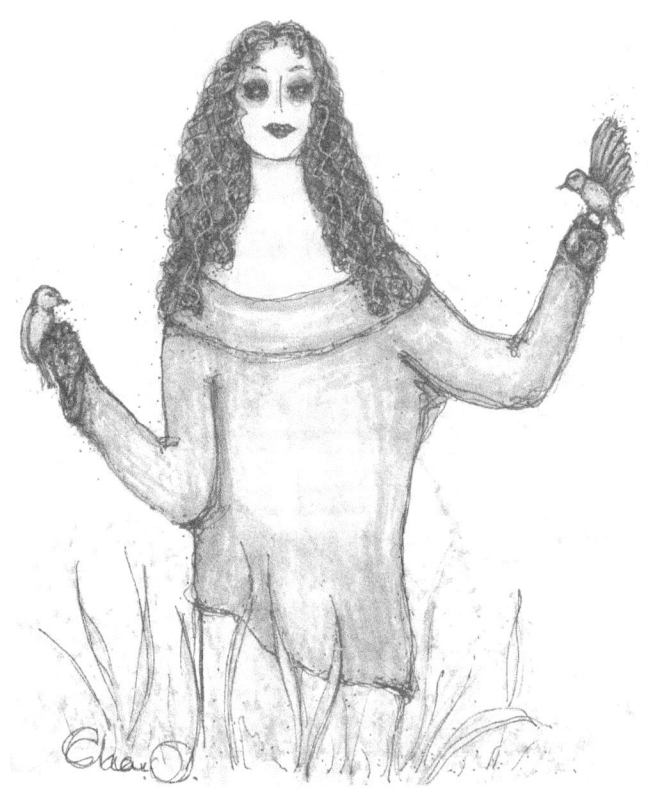

-Wild Flower-

-Wild Flower-

How a weed grows

I long to

Rest my mind

I spend my day

Open the gate

To sooth my heart ache

I will flourish

In a secret garden

Acceptance Phase

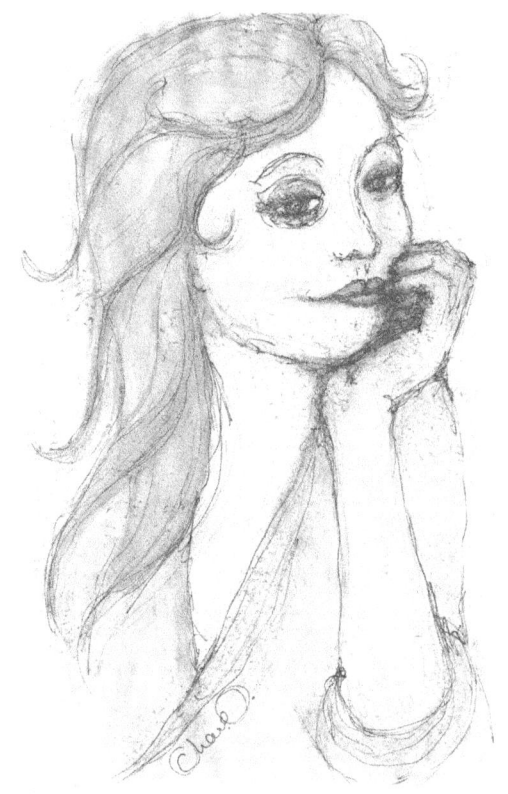

-Thinking Now-

-Thinking Now-

Time runs faster

Days are shorter

I have to cherish

What is left

Body weakened

But my spirit is fire

Fueled by life

I take charge

Transform Phase

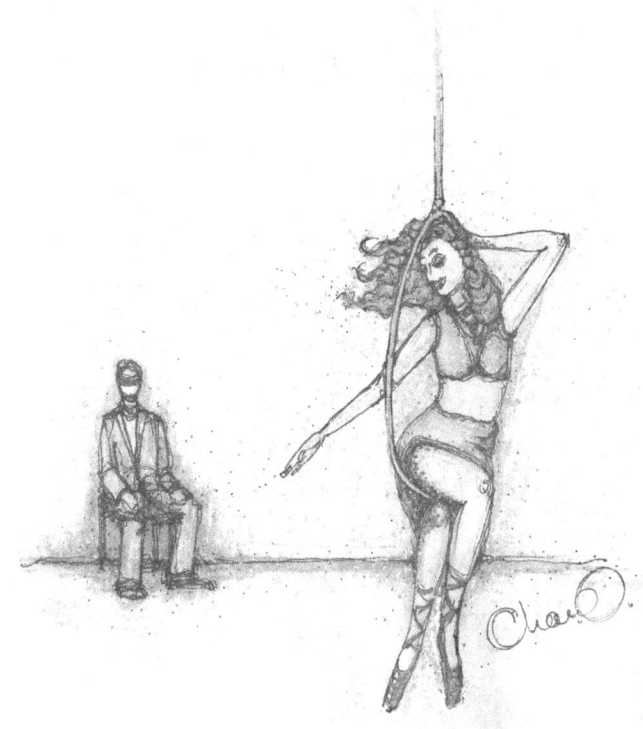

-Swing Me-

-Swing Me-

Into dull skies

Hold me

Amongst lightening stars

Heavenly showers

Forsaken memories

Live like this

Laughing light

Back and forth

Brief lasting happiness

Enlightenment Phase

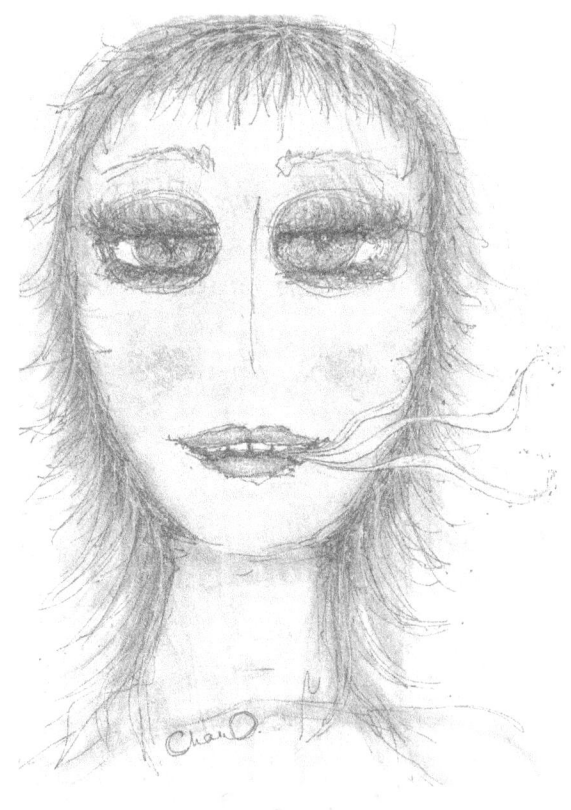

-My Breath-

-My Breath-

Light breathing

Misty moist

Dry inhale

Warm exhale

Mind wandering journey

Meeting the dimensional shift

On my monoxide fumes

I enter

Inspirational Theme

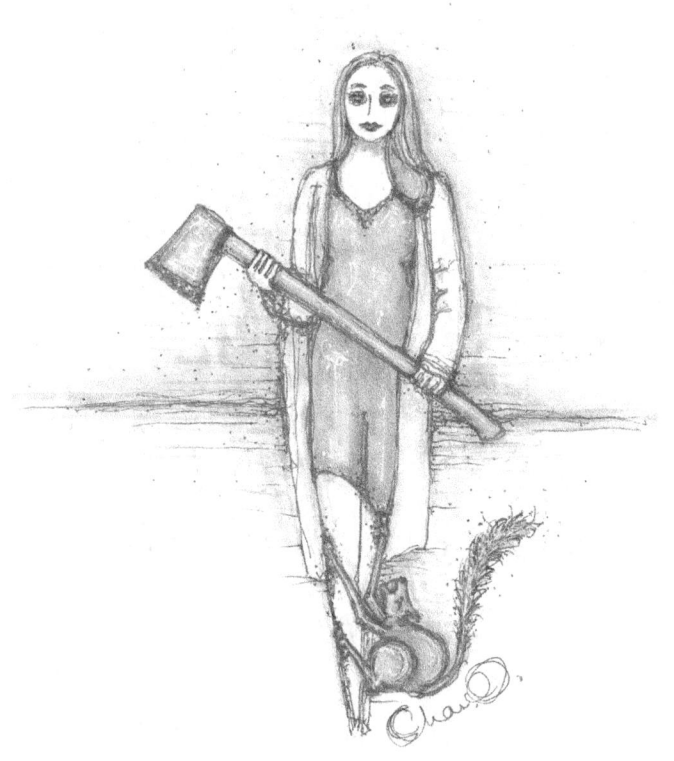

-Psyche Killer-

-Psyche Killer-

Make a stand

Constructed ideas

Beauty by society

Lethal warning

Reflection in the mirror

Take a selfie

May be distorted

Filters involved

Fake your future

Or get a life

Innocent Phase

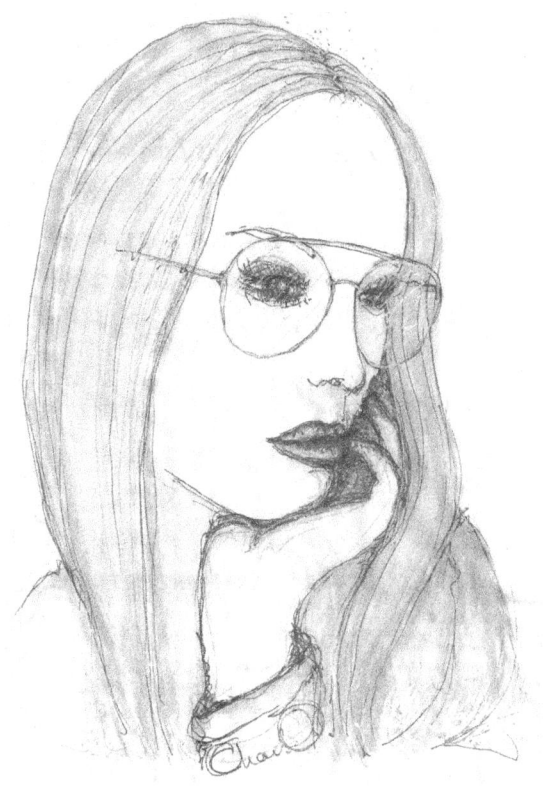

-You Think-

-You Think-

It is not

What others see

You become

What you feel

You create

From your mind

You attract

What you imagine

Learner Phase

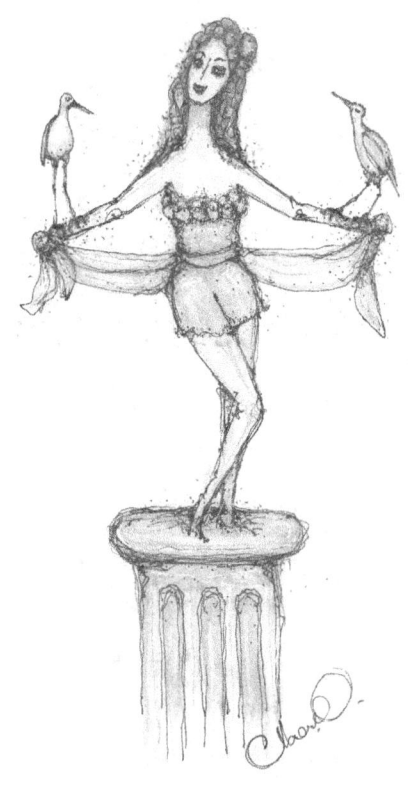

-Trophy Wife-

-Trophy Wife-

Up on a pedestal

Takes a lot of work

To keep up a façade

Drop the idea

Of becoming someone

You are already

A masterpiece

Only to know it

And realize

Seducer Phase

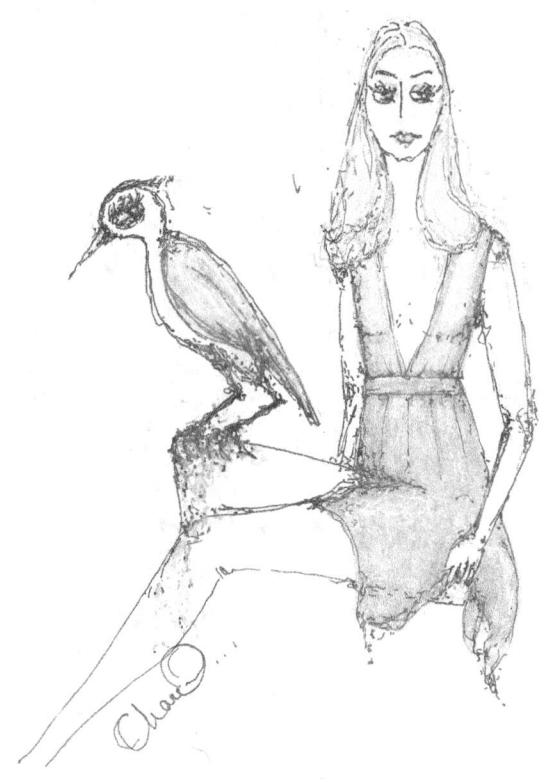

-I See-

-I See-

You are looking

Liking the attention

Young and careless

Emotions explode

Taunting

Teasing

A tickle deep inside

I see your look

Explorer Phase

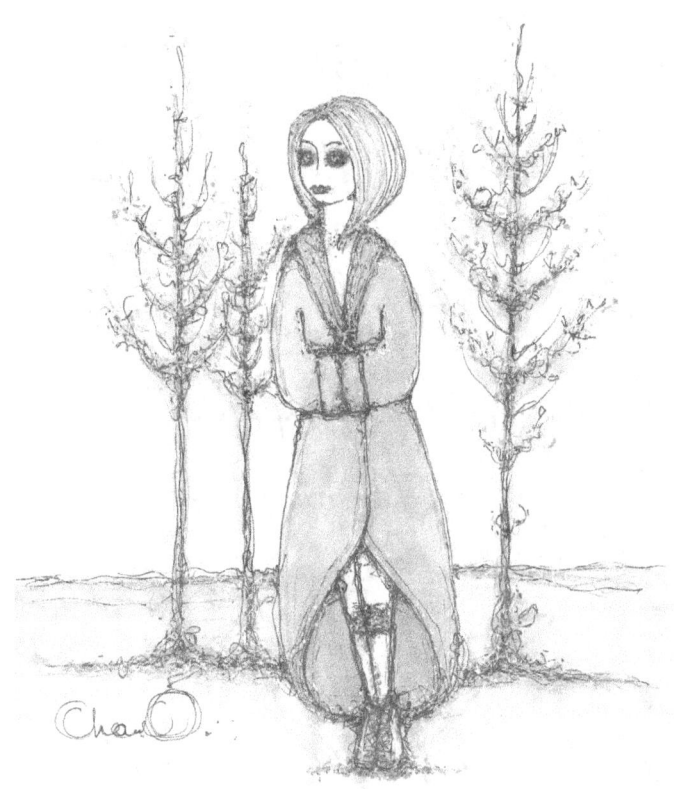

-Bloody Knees-

-Bloody Knees-

Ice cold night

Stumbles on

A slippery path

Why is the ground

Attacking me

Hands burning

The snow so sharp

Dangerous party gifts

Must focus my gaze

Please get me home

Lover Phase

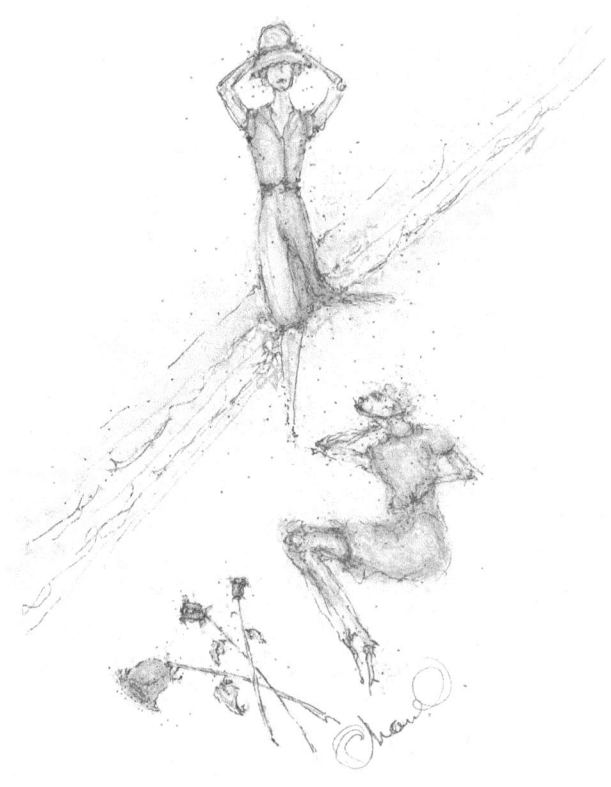

-Fragile Bones-

-Fragile Bones-

Paper thin

Skin like glass

Over land and sea

Frosted blue

Eyes seeking

A shining star

Gazing through fog

Onto the horizon

Lips quiver

A breathless whisper

From the eastern shore

Soft goodbyes

Nurturer Phase

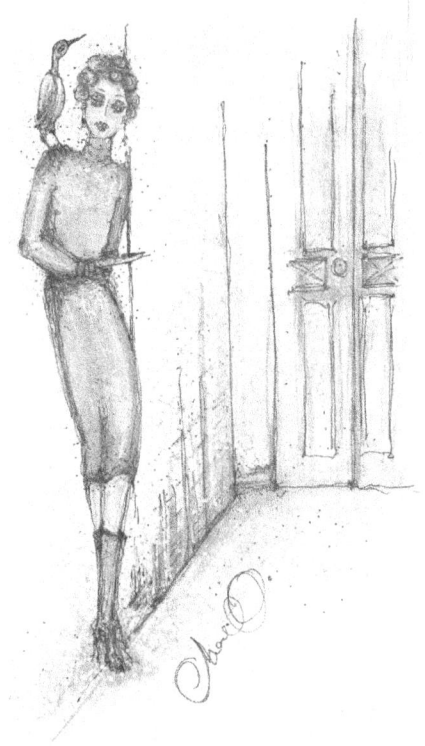

-Hypocrite Go-

-Hypocrite Go-

Say as you do

Do as you say

Only your life

Is yours

How does the shoe fit

For others understand

Individual desire

Do not judge

But yourself

Acceptance Phase

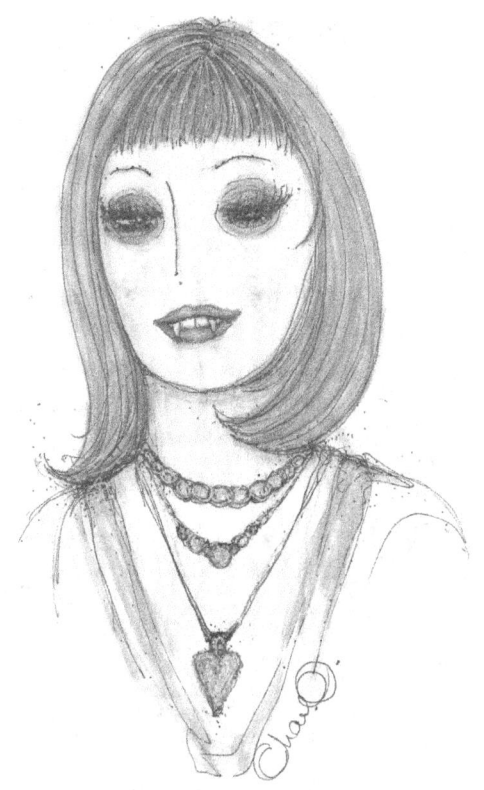

-Rebel Roar-

-Rebel Roar-

Youth unnerved

Wild at heart

Edgy expressions

Flaunting flesh

Baring teeth

Ruby jeweled neck

Choking restraints

Un chain her

Transform Phase

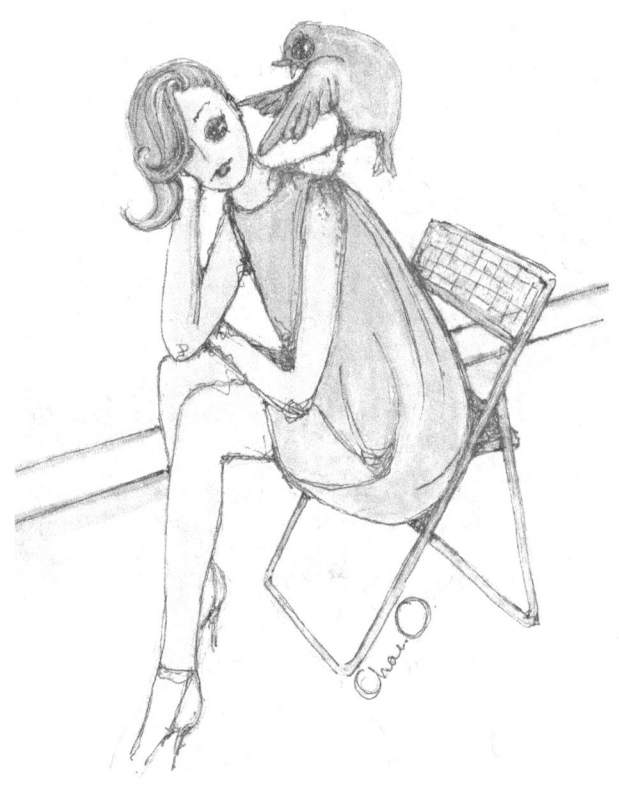

-Bring Light-

-Bring Light-

Darkness

Do not leave

I need you

How else

Can I get better

Opposites attract

You need me

Keep me sane

Shadow world

Make me

A better person

Enlightenment Phase

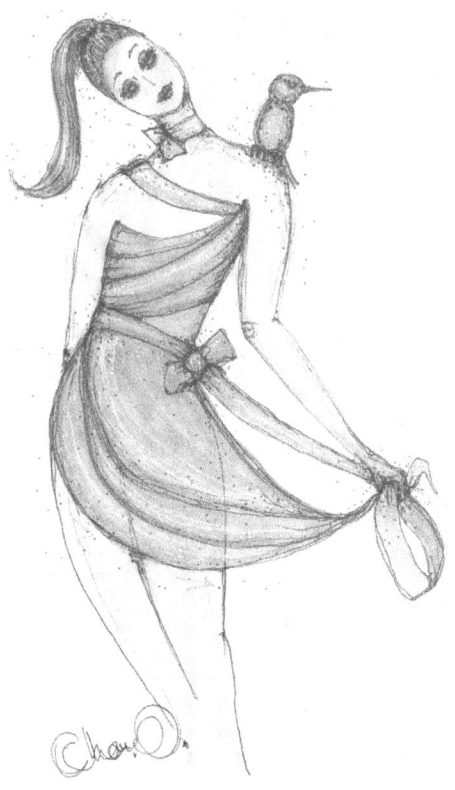

-Ribbons Bind-

-Ribbons Bind-

Her approval no more

The bow untied

My blue heart

Is moving on

A bruised soul

From your restraints

Rejoice everything

I have come undone

About the Author

Charlotta is a native of Sweden that has lived in California for the past 30 years. She has waited her whole life to be able to finally start focus on her art and to share it with the world. Since childhood she enjoyed crafting and writing with her grandparents and has always dreamed of using her abilities to inspire and share her experiences through art. Her work is focused on her life experiences and she hopes it will encourage her readers to view life in a new perspective. She feels her work would have a positive response due to its targeted clientele of art lovers, truth seekers and life rebels of all ages, countries and believes. Her art will provide encouragement and inspiration especially for younger people to understand the trials of life and how to overcome. She is working on her second book right now and there is more waiting to be developed after that. She also wants her artwork to be used in other mediums such as sale of original art, printed art, limited collection books, home décor, novelty items, clothing and textiles to further share her message.

For purchase of this book or other books,

original art, reproductions and gifts.

Please visit

www.ateljerose.com